THE MINIATURE BOOK OF

TOMATOES

CRESCENT BOOKS
New York

Published by Salamander Books Limited
129-137 York Way, London N7 9LG, United Kingdom

© Salamander Books Ltd., 1991

This 1991 edition published by Crescent Books, distributed by
Outlet Book Company, Inc., a Random House Company,
225 Park Avenue South, New York, New York 10003.

Printed and bound in Belgium

ISBN 0-517-06112-0

87654321

CREDITS

RECIPES BY: *Mary Cadogan, Linda Fraser, Kerenza Harries,
Janice Murfitt, Cecilia Norman, Lorna Rhodes, and Louise Steele*

PHOTOGRAPHY BY: *David Gill, Paul Grater, Sue Jorgensen,
Alan Newnham, Jon Stewart and Alister Thorpe*

DESIGN BY: *Tim Scott*

TYPESET BY: *The Old Mill*

COLOR SEPARATION BY: *P&W Graphics, Pte. Ltd.*

PRINTED IN BELGIUM BY: *Proost International Book Production,
Turnhout, Belgium*

$\mathcal{C}$ONTENTS

CHILLED TOMATO SOUP   8

GLOBE ARTICHOKES IN TOMATO DRESSING   10

TOMATO & ZUCCHINI SOUP   12

ITALIAN TOMATO SALAD   14

TOMATO-ORANGE SOUP   16

LAMB & WALNUT BALLS   18

PASTA WITH CLAMS   20

MEXICAN KEBABS   22

SPICED CHICKEN THIGHS   24

SCALLOPS & CREAMY TOMATO SAUCE   26

TOMATO SALAD   28

TOMATO & BASIL MAYONNAISE   30

LOBSTER PARCELS   32

CHEESY STUFFED TOMATOES   34

PICKLED VEGETABLE MEDLEY   36

TOMATO KUCHUMBER   38

TOMATO & RED BELL PEPPER RELISH   40

CLAMS WITH TWO SAUCES   42

TUNA-STUFFED TOMATOES   44

$\mathcal{C}$HILLED TOMATO SOUP

2 lbs ripe tomatoes, chopped
3 green onions, chopped
½ red bell pepper, seeded, chopped
2 garlic cloves, crushed
2 cups vegetable stock
1 teaspoon sugar
2 tablespoons chopped fresh basil
¼ cup crème fraiche or plain yogurt
Salt and pepper to taste
1 avocado and snipped chives to garnish

*I*n a large saucepan, place tomatoes, green onions, bell pepper, stock, garlic and sugar. Bring to a boil, then reduce the heat and simmer 15 minutes. Cool. In a food processor fitted with a metal blade, or a blender, process contents of pan, then press through a nylon sieve into a bowl. Cover and refrigerate 2 hours. Stir in basil and crème fraiche or yogurt and season with salt and pepper.

For the garnish, halve avocado. Pit, peel and slice. Divide soup between 6 cold bowls, float avocado slices on top and sprinkle with chives. *Makes 6 servings.*

$\mathcal{G}$LOBE ARTICHOKES IN TOMATO DRESSING

4 large globe artichokes, stalks and damaged leaves removed,
and tops trimmed
2 tablespoons tomato paste
1/4 cup olive oil
2/3 cup dry white wine
2/3 cup water
1 small onion, finely chopped
1 garlic clove, crushed
1 teaspoon chopped oregano
2 sprigs of thyme
2 ripe tomatoes, peeled and chopped
Salt and pepper to taste
lemon wedges and oregano sprigs to garnish

*P*lace artichokes in a large pan of boiling salted water, return to boil and cook 15 minutes. Drain, rinse and dry. For the sauce, in a saucepan, combine ingredients, bring to a boil, then cover and simmer 10 minutes, stirring occasionally. Discard thyme sprigs. Place artichokes in sauce, cover and simmer 30 minutes. Remove artichokes to a plate; cool. Boil sauce, uncovered, 5 minutes; cool. Remove hairy chokes and scoop out hairs from artichokes; discard. Place artichokes on 4 plates. Pour sauce around. Cover and refrigerate until required. Garnish with lemon wedges and oregano. *Makes 4 servings.*

TOMATO & ZUCCHINI SOUP

2 tablespoons butter
1 medium-size onion, finely chopped
1 garlic clove, crushed
12 oz zucchini, coarsely grated
2½ cups vegetable stock
1 (14-oz) can chopped tomatoes
2 tablespoons chopped fresh mixed herbs, if desired
Salt and pepper to taste
¼ cup whipping cream and fresh basil leaves to garnish

*I*n a large saucepan, melt butter. Add onion and cook until soft but not coloured. Stir in garlic and zucchini and cook, stirring occasionally, 4 to 5 minutes. Add stock and tomatoes with juice, and bring to a boil. Reduce heat and simmer 15 minutes. Stir in herbs, if desired, and season with salt and pepper. Serve garnished with spoonfuls of whipping cream and fresh basil. *Makes 4 servings.*

$\mathcal{I}$TALIAN TOMATO SALAD

2 large beefsteak tomatoes, sliced
6 oz mozzarella cheese, sliced
1 small red onion, sliced, separated into rings
Salt and black pepper to taste
¼ cup extra-virgin olive oil
1 tablespoon fresh basil leaves
1 tablespoon pine nuts

*O*n 4 individual plates, arrange alternate slices of tomato and mozzarella in a circle. Place onion rings in center. Sprinkle salt and pepper over, then drizzle with olive oil. To serve, sprinkle with basil and pine nuts. *Makes 4 servings.*

NOTE: *Choose firm tomatoes — ripe if to be eaten immediately — or a little under-ripe for eating in a few days.*

$\mathcal{T}$OMATO-ORANGE SOUP

1 medium-size orange
1 tablespoon sunflower oil
1 small onion, chopped
1 garlic clove, crushed
1½ lbs ripe tomatoes, coarsely chopped
2 cups chicken stock
1 teaspoon chopped fresh basil leaves
1 teaspoon sugar
Salt and pepper to taste
¼ cup whipping cream, whipped, to garnish

*U*sing a potato peeler, remove 4 strips of peel from orange; reserve. Grate remaining peel and squeeze juice. Heat oil in a large saucepan. Add onion and garlic and cook over low heat, stirring occasionally, until softened but not colored. Stir in grated orange peel and tomatoes and cook over medium heat until tomatoes are soft, about 5 minutes. Add stock, basil and sugar, cover and simmer 15 minutes. Cut reserved peel in thin strips; cook in simmering water 3 minutes. Drain then dry on a paper towel. In a food processor or blender, process soup to puree, press through a sieve and return to rinsed pan. Add orange juice and reheat gently. Season with salt and pepper. Serve garnished with whipped cream and orange strips. *Makes 4 servings.*

𝓛AMB &
WALNUT BALLS

8 oz lamb fillet, cut up
1 shallot
1 cup soft bread crumbs
1 egg
2 teaspoons fresh rosemary
1 teaspoon salt and ground black pepper
5 pickled walnuts, chopped
All-purpose flour
1 onion, finely chopped
1 clove garlic, crushed
3 large tomatoes, peeled, seeded, chopped
1 tablespoon chopped fresh basil
Oil for frying

*I*n a food processor fitted with a metal blade, finely chop lamb. Add shallot, bread crumbs, egg, rosemary and season. Process until smooth. Take 1 teaspoonful of meat mixture. Using a little flour, form into a ball, enclosing a piece of pickled walnut in center. Repeat to make 35 to 40 balls. For the sauce, in a small saucepan mix onion, garlic and tomatoes. Bring to a boil, then boil rapidly, stirring, until thick. Stir in basil. Heat a small saucepan half-filled with oil to 350F (175C). Lightly brown meatballs 2 to 3 minutes. Drain and serve with warmed sauce. *Makes 4 servings.*

$\mathscr{P}$ASTA WITH CLAMS

1 red bell pepper, charred under hot grill
2 eggs beaten
1 tablespoon olive oil
2 cups bread flour
pinch of salt
¼ cup unsalted butter
1 onion, finely chopped
1 (14-oz) can chopped tomatoes
Pinch of sugar
Salt and pepper, to taste
1 lb clams, cooked and shells removed
2 teaspoons chopped tarragon
3 tablespoons chopped parsley

*W*rap red pepper in foil, cool then peel and discard seeds. Puree. Mix with egg and oil. Combine flour and salt on work surface and form a well in center. Pour in pepper mixture, gradually mix in flour to make a soft dough. Knead until smooth. Roll out thinly, then roll up and slice into strips. For the sauce, in a medium-size saucepan, melt butter, add onion and soften. Stir in tomatoes, sugar, salt and pepper. Simmer 20 minutes. Puree, then return to pan. Put clams, tarragon and parsley in sauce and warm. In a large pan of boiling salted water, cook pasta, 3 to 4 minutes. Drain. *Makes 4 servings.*

MEXICAN KEBABS

¾ lb boneless trimmed beef sirloin steak, cut in 1-inch cubes
¾ lb pork loin tenderloin, cut in 1-inch cubes
1 large red bell pepper, seeded, cut in 1-inch cubes
1 large green bell pepper, seeded, cut in 1-inch cubes
MARINADE:
2 fresh green chili peppers, seeded
1 (8-oz) can tomatoes
1 (8-oz) can pimentos, drained
2 tablespoons fresh lemon juice
2 tablespoons olive oil
1 garlic clove, crushed
1 teaspoon ground turmeric
½ to 1 teaspoon salt
½ teaspoon freshly ground black pepper
Fresh flat-leaf parsley sprigs to garnish

*F*or the marinade, in a food processor fitted with a metal blade, or a blender, process all the ingredients. Pour into a medium-size saucepan and simmer, stirring occasionally, until reduced by ½. Pour into bowl; cool. Stir in meat and bell peppers. Cover tightly and refrigerate 12 hours, turning occasionally. Lift meat and bell peppers from marinade. Thread alternately onto skewers. Grill, turning frequently and basting with marinade, about 20 minutes. Garnish. *Makes 5-6 servings.*

$\mathcal{S}$PICED
CHICKEN THIGHS

8 chicken thighs, skinned
MARINADE
1 (8 oz) can tomatoes, drained
6 teaspoons tomato paste
2 tablespoons chili sauce
2 teaspoons sugar
1 tablespoon Garam Masala
2 tablespoons light soy sauce
1 (2-in) piece fresh ginger root, grated
2 cloves garlic, crushed
Juice of 1 lime and 1 lemon
Twists of lime and lemon to garnish

Cut 2 or 3 slashes in meaty part of chicken thighs; place in a shallow non-metal ovenproof dish.

For the marinade, in a food processor fitted with a metal blade, or a blender, process all ingredients together. Pour over chicken, turn to coat evenly, cover and let stand in a cool place 2 to 3 hours. Cook, uncovered in an oven preheated to 375F (190C), basting occasionally, until flesh is tender and juices run clear, about 45-50 minutes. Serve garnished with lime and lemon twists. *Makes 4 servings.*

$\mathcal{S}$CALLOPS & CREAMY TOMATO SAUCE

1 lb shelled sea scallops
1 tablespoon sunflower oil
1 small leek, white part only, finely chopped
¼ cup dry vermouth
¼ cup dry white wine
3 ripe tomatoes, peeled, seeded, finely chopped
⅔ cup fromage frais or crème fraiche
8 basil leaves, torn
Salt and pepper, to taste
Basil sprigs to garnish

*R*inse scallops, discard any dark strands, pat dry with paper towels. In a skillet, heat oil, add leek and cook until softened, about 5 minutes. Stir in vermouth and wine, boil, reduce heat and simmer 2 minutes. Add scallops, cover and cook until opaque and just firm, 3 to 4 minutes. Using a slotted spoon, remove and keep warm. Reduce cooking juices to 2 tablespoons by boiling. Reduce heat, add tomatoes, heat through, then add fromage frais or crème fraiche, and basil. Heat through gently; do not boil. Season with salt and pepper. Divide sauce between 4 warmed plates, arrange scallops in center and garnish with basil sprigs. *Makes 4 servings.*

TOMATO SALAD

1 lb firm-ripe tomatoes, thinly sliced
1 teaspoon sugar
Salt and black pepper to taste
6 tablespoons virgin olive oil
2 tablespoons white wine vinegar
1 tablespoon snipped chives

*A*rrange tomato slices on serving plate. Sprinkle with sugar, salt and pepper. In a small bowl, stir together oil and vinegar. Drizzle over tomatoes. Sprinkle with chives, cover and refrigerate at least 1 hour. *Makes 4 servings.*

VARIATION: *Sprinkle salad with finely chopped onion or shredded fresh basil instead of chives. Alternatively, for Garlic Dressing, add 2 crushed cloves garlic and replace chives with 3 teaspoons chopped fresh parsley. Mix until thoroughly combined.*

$\mathcal{T}$OMATO & BASIL MAYONNAISE

3 medium-size tomatoes, peeled, seeded and finely chopped
2 tablespoons plus 2 teaspoons fresh basil, finely chopped
1 tablespoon snipped fresh chives
1 garlic clove, crushed
1 teaspoon superfine sugar
⅔ cup mayonnaise
2 tablespoons plain yogurt

*I*n a medium-sized bowl, using a wooden spoon, mix tomatoes, basil, chives, garlic and sugar. Carefully stir in mayonnaise and yogurt until evenly blended. Cover and refrigerate until needed. *Makes 1 cup.*

NOTE: *Tomato & Basil Mayonnaise can be used to coat rice or pasta salad or to toss cooked mixed vegetables. Alternatively, serve as an accompaniment to lamb or chicken kebabs.*

$\mathscr{L}$OBSTER PARCELS

1/4 cup butter
2 tablespoons chopped watercress
Salt and pepper, to taste
8 sheets filo pastry
Melted butter for brushing
6 oz cooked lobster meat, roughly chopped
1 lb tomatoes, peeled, seeded and chopped
1 teaspoon tomato paste
Pinch of sugar
8 to 10 basil leaves, chopped
Snipped chives and lemon twists to garnish

*F*or the sauce, in a saucepan, simmer tomatoes, tomato paste and sugar until thickened, about 15 to 20 minutes. Meanwhile, in a bowl, beat together butter, watercress, salt and pepper. Brush 1 sheet filo pastry with melted butter, fold in 1/2 and brush again. Place a little lobster meat near 1 short edge and spread with watercress butter. Roll up pastry to enclose filling, tucking in ends to form a parcel. Place on a greased baking sheet and brush top with melted butter. Repeat with remaining filo, lobster and butter. Bake in an oven preheated to 400F (205C) until golden, about 15 minutes. To serve, stir basil into sauce, arrange 2 parcels on each plate, add some sauce. Sprinkle sauce with chives and garnish. *Makes 4 servings.*

CHEESY STUFFED TOMATOES

8 tomatoes
2 tablespoons vegetable oil
1 small onion, finely chopped
1 garlic clove, crushed
1 (1-inch) piece fresh gingerroot, grated
1 teaspoon ground cumin
½ teaspoon ground turmeric
½ teaspoon red (cayenne) pepper
2 teaspoons ground coriander
½ cup fresh farmers cheese
¼ cup shredded Cheddar cheese
Salt to taste
1 tablespoon chopped cilantro (fresh coriander)

*S*lice the top from each tomato. Scoop out flesh and discard seeds from tomatoes; chop flesh and reserve. In a small skillet, heat oil, add onion and cook until soft, about 5 minutes. Stir in garlic and gingerroot, cook 1 minute, add cumin, turmeric, cayenne and coriander and cook another minute. Stir in tomato flesh, cook 5 minutes. Off the heat, stir in farmers cheese and ½ Cheddar cheese. Season. Spoon into tomato shells, sprinkle remaining Cheddar cheese on tomato tops and bake in an oven preheated to 375F (190C), 10 to 15 minutes. Sprinkle with cilantro. *Makes 4 servings.*

$\mathcal{P}$ICKLED VEGETABLE MEDLEY

1 cucumber, peeled, thinly sliced
8 zucchini, trimmed, thinly sliced
1 lb pickling onions, peeled, thinly sliced
1 lb red and green bell peppers, seeded, thinly sliced
1 lb green or red tomatoes, peeled, seeded, thinly sliced
3 tablespoons salt
Red bell pepper rings and tarragon sprigs to garnish
2 cups light-brown sugar
1 teaspoon celery seeds
1 teaspoon turmeric
1 teaspoon ground mace
1 tablespoon plus 1 teaspoon mustard seeds
2½ cups tarragon, cider or wine vinegar

*I*n a large bowl, layer the vegetables, sprinkling salt between each layer. Cover and refrigerate 3 hours. Drain vegetables and rinse well under cold running water.

For the spiced vinegar, in a stainless steel or enamel saucepan, mix all ingredients. Over low heat, stir with wooden spoon until sugar dissolves. Bring to a boil and boil 3 minutes. Add vegetables, return to a boil, stirring occasionally. Cook 1 minute. Spoon into serving bowl. Serve hot or cold, garnished with bell pepper rings and tarragon sprigs. *Makes 10-12 servings.*

TOMATO KUCHUMBER

12 oz cherry tomatoes, quartered
6 green onions
1 green chili, seeded, chopped
1 tablespoon lemon juice
Salt and red (cayenne) pepper to taste
2 tablespoons chopped cilantro (fresh coriander)

*P*ut tomatoes into serving bowl. Cut green onions diagonally into long, thin slices. Sprinkle over tomatoes, add chili and gently mix together. Sprinkle with remaining ingredients. Cover and refrigerate 30 minutes. *Makes 4-6 servings.*

NOTE: *The seeds of the chili can be left in, if preferred, to make this dish very hot.*

TOMATO & RED BELL PEPPER RELISH

4 large ripe tomatoes, finely chopped
1 small red bell pepper, cored, seeded, finely chopped
1 small green bell pepper, cored, seeded, finely chopped
1 large onion, finely chopped
2 teaspoons salt
½ cup dark-brown sugar
⅔ cup malt vinegar
½ teaspoon sweet paprika
Fresh flat-leaf parsley sprigs to garnish

*I*n a large saucepan, combine all ingredients. Bring to a boil, reduce heat and simmer, stirring frequently, until mixture is thick, about 1 hour. Spoon into a large sterilized jar. Cover with a sterilized lid. Cool. Refrigerate 1 to 2 weeks before serving. To serve, spoon into a bowl and garnish with parsley sprigs. *Makes about 2 cups.*

$\mathcal{C}$LAMS
WITH TWO SAUCES

4 lbs mussels in shells
½ cup dry white wine
TOMATO BASIL SAUCE
1 (14 oz) can chopped tomatoes
1 tablespoon tomato paste
2 teaspoons torn basil leaves
1 teaspoon chopped fresh oregano
Pinch of sugar
Salt and pepper, to taste
FENNEL SAUCE
2 tablespoons butter
1 leek, finely chopped
1 fennel bulb, finely chopped
¼ cup whipping cream

*I*n a large saucepan, over high heat, cook mussels in wine until the shells open, 4 to 6 minutes. Drain; discard any closed mussels or empty shells. Keep warm. For the Tomato Basil Sauce, in a saucepan, combine all ingredients. Simmer until thick and smooth, about 15 minutes. For the Fennel Sauce, in a pan, melt butter. Add vegetables and cook until softened, about 5 minutes. Stir in cream, simmer 2 minutes. Puree and season. Place mussels in their half shells on plates, and fill shells alternately with the sauces. *Makes 4-6 servings.*

TUNA-STUFFED TOMATOES

4 medium beef tomatoes
Salt and pepper
4 (1-in) thick slices white bread, crusts removed
1/3 cup butter, mixed with fresh herbs and crushed garlic, to taste
185 g (6-oz) can tuna chunks, drained
1 teaspoon bottled pesto sauce
1 egg, separated
1 teaspoon finely grated Parmesan cheese
Basil sprigs to garnish

Slice tops from tomatoes. Using a teaspoon scoop out seeds and flesh. Let tomatoes stand upside down on paper towels. Using a 2 inch cutter, remove centers from bread slices. Make centers into 2 tablespoons bread crumbs. Melt ¼ cup garlic and herb butter; brush over both sides of each bread slice. Place on a baking sheet and stand a tomato in hole in each slice. Melt remaining butter, stir in tuna, pesto sauce, prepared bread crumbs and egg yolk. Whip egg white until stiff. Lightly fold into tuna mixture then fill tomatoes. Sprinkle tops with Parmesan cheese. Bake in an oven preheated to 400F (205C) until filling is risen and golden and bread is crisp, about 12 to 15 minutes. Garnish with basil sprigs. *Makes 4 servings.*